the meandering muse

uncommon views of everyday things

Katherine Mayfield

First print edition published by The Essential Word Press.

Also by Katherine Mayfield

The Box of Daughter: Healing the Authentic Self

*Stand Your Ground: How to Cope with
a Dysfunctional Family and Recover from Trauma*

*Dysfunctional Families:
The Truth Behind the Happy Family Facade*

*Dysfunctional Families:
Healing the Legacy of Toxic Parents*

Bullied: Why You Feel Bad Inside and What to Do About It

The Box of Daughter & Other Poems

The Last Visit

Acting A to Z

Smart Actors, Foolish Choices

Contents

Random Musings and a Bit of Soapboxing

Introduction

Over the twenty or so years that I've been writing, I've collected many bits and pieces on all kinds of subjects, written in inspired moments, during writing groups, and when I'm half-asleep, all of which I subsequently stuffed into a folder for future use.

At a recent point in my journey of rediscovering myself and my love of life, my Muse decided that all of these pieces should be brought out from the darkness of forgetting into the light of possibility and enjoyment.

I offer these pieces for your own enjoyment and enlightenment. There are humorous essays, poems, and stories mixed in along with a little soapboxing about the state of the world and a few flights of fancy that prompted a little Muse-snickering as they emerged.

Some of them have been published elsewhere online, in local newspapers in Massachusetts, or included in my blog on dysfunctional families at www.TheBoxofDaughter.com. Some are simply happy to be resurrected from the cold darkness of my filing cabinet.

I encourage you to continue on your own journey of self-discovery, wherever it may lead you, and to trust the truth that's inside of you over the illusions that pervade the world. And if you like to write, the list of writing prompts that generated these meanderings is included at the end.

BTW, I'd like to thank Dave Barry for his inspiration. Every time I read one of his books, my Muse gets really excited and starts pouring out ideas. Thanks, Dave. You're a genius!

The Blender Effect

This week, I feel like I'm living in a blender. Everything is whirling and twirling in a messy goo of missed appointments, half-baked emotions, unexpressed desires, and fretful annoyances. I bend uneasily under the heavy weight of my calendar, stumbling only half-effectively from one task to the next, while the clock continues tsk-ing out its count of the seconds I no longer have available to get too many things done.

The creatures on my to-do list are whining with dismay at having been left alone too long, each one moaning louder in my mind when I attend to another, in the hopes that it will become the next accomplishment.

And the accomplishments slide under my feet like a muddy, uneven treadmill, sometimes so fast that I don't even notice; and while the accomplishment treadmill chugs tiredly onward beneath my feet, the guilt-for-not-getting-enough-done movie plays over and over in my head, following the endless dog-eared loop that traps nearly every average American citizen.

The world is tilting, and I feel as if everything is about to slide off—all that I think I know about myself and life is sliding sideways into a huge confusing jumble of mistakes and missteps and misunderstandings, pushed over the edge by the scorekeeping judge of my general ability to cope with life, who lives in my head and always knows where my most tender vulnerabilities lie. I look at the smoldering, sodden heap of what

I thought I knew, and the sigh that starts in my brain glides slowly and steadily all the way down to my toes.

Perhaps spirituality is not always about reaching for the clouds or finding inner peace. Sometimes it's about scrabbling down into the dark earth of life, coping with the Blender Effect without resistance, and knowing that everything will still turn out okay in the end.

The Long-Awaited Rebirth

My hummingbird has returned. At last, it's springtime! As I was sitting on the back porch the other day, I saw it hovering near where its feeder hung last summer. For a few glorious moments, it perched in the lilac bush not five feet away from me before flitting off, making a quick detour around the regular bird feeder to make sure I knew what it was asking for. At long last, spring is here! So far it's a pretty nice one, and we certainly deserve it after what we've been through.

Spring is springing, birds are singing, and suddenly it's very obvious how much yard work I didn't get to before the first snow fell last fall. Dead leaves and broken branches vie with daffodils and hyacinths for my attention. And the scourge of spring, the wasp, has been busy at my house. In fact, I've already had one *in* my house.

I opened both the front and back doors, and politely invited the wasp to fly right out. I made waving motions with my arms; then turned on the fan to try and blow it out; then went to the door and called, "Wasp! Wasp! This way!", then pleaded, "Please leave—you'll really like it outside better!"

Nothing worked. Until I made a fabulous discovery (this is my Homeowner's Tip of the Week): I went outside and picked a daffodil, attached it to the end of a broomstick with a rubber band, and slowly moved it up close to the wasp. (Note: using a broomstick hopefully makes it look like any misfortune is the broomstick's fault, not the human's.) Bless its heart, it climbed right onto the daffodil, and I carried it safely outside before running back in to close the doors. I don't know why I picked a daffodil, except that the wasp wouldn't get on the broomstick with nothing on it, and honey didn't work either.

I mused briefly on how many things I would have tried before giving up if the daffodil hadn't worked, but then I really don't like wasps. I suppose I would have given up eventually and simply sprayed it, but I don't like those sprays almost as much as I don't like wasps. I thanked the daffodil profusely, placed it in a vase, and paid homage to it once a day until it passed away.

Unfortunately, after a few weeks I ran out of daffodils, after which I discovered that bananas also work. I'm pleased that nobody with a video camera was around for that discovery, since I'd feel really stupid being seen on America's Funniest Home Videos running around with a banana tied to the end of a long stick (I don't imagine that the wasp would show up on the film).

So at the risk of feeling foolish, which I do, I'm offering this banana tip to those of you who have been tearing your hair out because you have no daffodils to remove your wasps with.

Next year, I think I'll just get a can of wasp-spray.

Enjoy this glorious season of renewal, and make sure you have some daffodils and bananas handy as an important part of your Natural Wasp Elimination Program.

Lunar Disconnect

I am constantly amazed by the vast creative energy of the Universe. Even at 44, I'm still looking at things and going, "Wow! I didn't know it could do that!" and "So that's what that's for!" And I enjoy the discoveries just as much as I did when I was 4. I love living this way!

The other night, I was walking down by the lake, and spent a few moments gazing in wonder at the full moon. I thought, as I had many times before, how beautiful the moon is, lighting up the night sky and sending its lovely, gentle radiance across the landscape. So many beautiful things have yet another purpose besides simply providing beauty, and I began to wonder if there's a purpose to the moon.

We know that there's a purpose behind the sun: it creates those wonderful little Vitamin Ds in our bodies that help us to be healthy, and it makes plants grow. Up until my walk, I'd thought the moon was just for show.

Then I thought about how legend has it that people tend to be a little more wild and crazy during a full moon, and weird things occasionally happen. I've noticed that my cat needs to scamper and play more when the moon is full, and that I'm a bit more restless and energetic. I suppose that might be because the moons rules the tides, and since our bodies (and cats' bodies too, I imagine) are mostly water, the phases of the moon have our blood and tissues swinging back and forth just like the ocean tides. (Do our little cells smile with happiness because the tide is in? Is there more to eat then?) Sometimes our emotional tides seem to change with the changing cycles of the moon. And I started thinking that maybe the Creator purposefully made the moon exactly for that reason.

Everything seems to have a purpose: birds eat bugs; bugs carry pollen; even slugs provide a pure protein treat for birds. So why not the moon? Here's my theory:

The sun was created in order to benefit our physical bodies: to generate our Vitamin Ds; to help us grow plants and fruit, which give us needed vitamins; and to bring light to the daytime so we wouldn't stumble over things and hurt ourselves. What about the moon? My theory is that the moon was created expressly with the purpose of affecting our internal state, of helping us to keep things flowing emotionally. Why else would it be set up astronomically to wax and wane?

Sure, we enjoy the variety of seeing a little sliver of moon for a while, and then watching it grow into fullness and back again. But I think it was made on purpose to give an internal, emotional flow to our lives so that we would continue to grow and explore, to feel and express—just as the sun gives an external rhythm to our days and nights.

And what happened when the light bulb was invented? One change was that man could then light his office so that he could work later. And of course it brought light into a whole host of after-dinner family activities. But artificial lighting may have also caused Lunar Disconnect: that nagging sensation that we've become separated from our feelings, that we no longer know who we are inside, what we want, what we feel.

I say, let's save our lightbulbs for special occasions like parties and dances, and get reconnected with the moon. I for one would like to shine a little moonlight into the core of who I am and find out what's in there.

Will the Real Person Please Stand Up?

The other day I was ruminating on the fact that in the U.S., we start getting trained to enter the workforce when we're about five years old. Five years old! We go to kindergarten, and from day one, we're told what to do when. It all looks very innocent, of course—"Now we're going to sing all together," "Now we're going to go outside and play"—but in reality, we're getting trained practically right off the bat to do what Those Who Are in Charge tell us to do.

In my mind, this is probably one of the primary reasons that 27 million Americans are on antidepressants and 91,000 American therapists make pretty good livings. I have nothing against therapists—they have helped me overcome that early training to do everything the way everybody else wants me to do it, so that I can finally put myself in charge of my life and do what I came here to do, be who I came here to be.

But the pressure to conform begins early, as school officials focus on keeping kids in line, making them perform satisfactorily, and keeping them from expressing the beautiful, infinite diversity that the Creator has given to every member of humankind. I wonder sometimes how many kids become troublemakers because their natural creative energy is being stuffed violently into a rigid schedule filled with a never-ending list of shoulds and have-tos.

And then there are the Tests: as we go through more years in school, the Tests give us the message that we must Perform, that we must Live Up to the Standards Set by Others, that we must learn what They want us to learn and continue to Do What They Want Us to Do. By the time we graduate and get into the workforce, we're completely brainwashed to believe that We Must Follow Whoever is Telling Us What to Do Because We Really Don't Know Anything.

But what about the kids who don't do so well in school? Who knows why they don't do well? Perhaps, like Einstein, they don't Perform According to Standards because their minds hold the seeds of Incredible Ideas—of possibilities and potentials that could radically change the world for the better. But instead, they're labeled Below Average, or even Stupid—which is a probable eliminator of any Grand Creations they might come up with and any Helpful Contributions they could make to the world by using their Potential and pouring out their Originality.

I just wonder if the world has so many problems because we're teaching kids that they have to be like Everybody Else instead of like themselves, that they have to live up to a standard set by Someone with Different Inclinations, and sometimes even that they're not worth paying attention to.

If I Were in Charge, I would change the curriculum to include the following classes:

- What Do You Do Best?
- Life 101
- How Would You Fix These Problems?

- Money 101
- Your Fantasy of the Perfect World
- What Do You Think About These Situations?
- Emotions 101
- Creativity 101
- Who You Are Inside

Of course, kids would still need to learn to read, write, and do their numbers—but what good is Trigonometry to a kid who, if he put his mind to it, could come up with a solution to world hunger? Or an alternative to war?

Somewhere out there is a kid who could put an end to bullying the same way Martin Luther King, Jr. started a movement to end discrimination. But he's struggling with spelling and arithmetic instead of focusing on the potential within him. Somewhere, there's another Gandhi, who could finally bring peace to the world, but he doesn't excel in sports like his dad wants him to, so his self-esteem is too low to let himself believe that he could change the world.

I realize that I may be coming off as The One Who Has the Answer, and I apologize for that. I just wanted to try it once to see what it feels like.

Excuse me while I go back to Doing What I'm Supposed to Be Doing.

Manifesting Medical Miracles

And while I'm on the subject of Those Who Tell Us What to Do, I'd like to offer an idea to the medical community. Don't get me wrong—I have unending appreciation for doctors, nurses, and surgeons, some of whom helped me get over Lyme Disease and heal various afflictions and disorders over the years. Most in the medical community are very dedicated to providing top-quality healthcare, and a lot of us would actually be dead without them. So I'd like to thank them all.

But I have an idea that might help make things work even better. Recently, a friend of mine told me something I'd never known about him—that he was diagnosed with high cholesterol as a teenager, several decades before. He was told by his doctors that he'd never be able to eat entire lists of things, from dairy products to avocados to meat. All well and good—restrictions like these can help keep cholesterol down. But.

My problem is with the follow-up to a Diagnosis of any kind. We hear time and again that the body is its own best healer, and that we can manifest reality with our thoughts, so why not take a Diagnosis as simply a Message to Change Our Thinking about what's going on in our bodies?

For instance, if someone in the medical community had told my friend, "This Diagnosis is meant as a signal for you to *start thinking about lowering your cholesterol*," instead of immediately prescribing some medication with a bunch of chemicals in it right off the bat, which would throw even more of the body's systems out of whack. A Diagnosis could simply mean that we need to change our thinking about whatever is going on in our bodies.

Of course, this would cut Profits at Pharmaceutical Companies, who are responsible for all those ads for drugs, which always include messages like "Can cause kidney failure" and "Do not take if you have feet." But maybe those workers at Pharmaceutical Companies who are stuck on the merry-go-round of Following What Others Tell Them to Do would actually be relieved by a layoff, and could go on to fix the Social Security Problem.

Louise Hay was actually the pioneer of this idea. She wrote a wonderful book called *You Can Heal Your Life*, which postulates thought-patterns which she believed created certain diseases, along with new thought-patterns which could be instilled in order to heal each disease. I've used her book for decades, and found it to be extremely helpful in reducing my medical bills and helping myself to feel better.

I was so disappointed to discover when I got Lyme Disease that it wasn't included in Louise Hay's book. So, avid surfer that I am, I scoured the internet for information as to what I might have been thinking that caused the Universe to send this message of "Lyme Disease" to my body. The only thing I ever found was a medical abstract titled, "To Self-Express or Not to Self-Express," which was actually about the ability of the Lyme bacteria to gain a foothold in the body, but which absolutely, totally described the mental conundrum I was in at that particular point in my life. Finding that article really made me think about some of the choices I'd made.

Isn't it all very weird? I'm constantly amazed at the workings of the Universe.

So the next time you or someone you love gets a Diagnosis, try sending a message to your/his/her body that it's time to lower the cholesterol, or regulate the blood sugar more efficiently, or provide more insulin, heal the knee, or whatever is needed. It will certainly be cheaper than a prescription, and it might even work.

To Everything There is a Season

In the autumn, the thing I'm most grateful for is *rest*. As the holiday season wends its way into the busyness of my days, I'm grateful for friends and family, and that I have a house that I love, plenty to eat, and nearly always enough to pay the bills. But more than anything else, I offer my heartfelt thanks for time off during the holiday season.

I'm sure that sounds cynical, but the holidays always seem so busy, as if I'm running after myself trying to pick up where I left off, and I don't even know where that is. Is there some primordial part of my brain that still thinks I need to rush around storing food for the winter? Or is it the combination of get-it-done-before-winter-comes, getting ready for the holidays, and enjoying more social activities before it's too cold to go out?

I could learn something from the trees—they always seem to be on schedule. I read somewhere some time ago (don't ask my brain for the answer to that one) that the reason trees change color in the fall is that they are withdrawing their sap from the leaves to rest for the winter. Odd as it seems, leaves are always yellow, red, and gold—it's just that the green chlorophyll in the leaves covers up the color in the spring and summer. I think trees are pretty smart.

I'm ready to withdraw my sap myself, this time of year. I feel like an old bear wanting to go hide in my cave and hibernate. Even the landscape seems to change its personality for the winter—the trees, bereft of their adornment of leaves and showing us the bones of the world, scratch tiny lace patterns into the sky with their branches. And the lake by my house seems colder, more remote, its secrets even deeper and darker.

I think about how life might have been different a century or so ago. With only gas lamps, firelight, and moonlight to keep folks from bumping into things at night, they probably went to bed not too long after dark. They may have risen with the sun, but in winter, that meant they'd have been getting around 12 hours of sleep a night! Even with dinner and after-dinner cleanup, they probably got 9 or 10. And in the summer, maybe only 8, the current "norm." (I suppose you don't need so much in the summer anyway, because your body doesn't have to work to keep itself warm.) And who makes up these "norms" anyway? I'd like to know. They never seem to fit me.

I think the longer nights are Nature's way of telling us to slow down, rest, maybe even sleep a little more, curl up inside, and show our true colors. I wonder sometimes if our society logs more violent acts, more depression, more stress in part because we're not sleeping as much as our ancestors did.

And maybe the cold is a signal to get a little closer to each other, be a little warmer with each other.

So be thankful that during the holiday season, you can get close to those you love and take a nice nap after those Big Yummy Dinners. Happy Holidays!

Multitasking May Be Hazardous to Your Health

For years, I've prided myself on my multitasking abilities. I've learned to multitask like a pro on the job and in my life. The more things I can do at once, the more productive I feel. But recently I was brought up short when I discovered that my multitasking habit had gotten out of hand.

I was driving in an unfamiliar city, scanning the buildings for a particular address. When I found what I thought I was looking for, my multitasking skills took over, and I attempted to confirm the address on the building while simultaneously parking my car. Whoops.

A few seconds later, I found myself sitting with my right front tire hanging up on the curb, and a small dent where I had bumped into the parking meter. I did manage to confirm the address while I was damaging my car—I was in the right place, at least. A few passersby looked upon my blunder with disdain, and, mustering as much dignity as I could, I put the car into reverse and slowly backed down off the curb with a thud.

I was lucky there wasn't a cop nearby—I could just imagine his or her face when I said, "No, officer, I'm not drunk, I was just multitasking." I learned that day that multitasking skills are only good if you know how to control them.

I consistently have trouble on those days when I get home from work and realize that I need to do laundry. I decide that I will put the laundry in, and fix dinner while I wait. It seems simple enough when I start. But no matter how I try to time it, dinner always seems to be ready just as the washer finishes, and I have to choose between wrinkled shirts and a cold dinner. I'm lucky that the washer isn't in the kitchen, or I'd probably be using olive oil to clean my clothes and cooking dinner with detergent.

At least I don't have a cell phone. I sometimes wonder how many auto repair shops are getting rich off the cell phone boom.

And I often wonder if Attention Deficit Disorder and overdeveloped multitasking skills might be one and the same thing. My multitasking skills have helped me to be really good at starting a number of projects, sometimes even at the same time, but they aren't at all helpful in finishing any of them. I get into multitasking mode, work a little on this, and start a little of that, but never seem to get around to finishing the 4,324 things I already have going.

Maybe what I need to do is take my skills to a different level. I think I'll pick three projects and spend 10 minutes at a time on each of them, going back and forth, until they're finished. The only problem is, I'll probably find five new projects to start while I'm trying to finish those three.

Yes, those multitasking skills come in handy for so many things. But I think the most important multitasking skill to learn is how to turn it off and focus on one thing at a time.

Shortly after my multitasking parking mishap, I read that a 27-year-old woman was killed when she lost control of her car on an interstate highway. According to witnesses, she was applying makeup while she was driving.

I think I will continue to use my bathroom mirror, thank you. And I will remember from now on never to multitask while I'm driving, or around anything electrical with coffee in my hand. Wow, that could really wake me up! I'd rather not find out what it would be like, thank you. I think I will slow down and do one thing at a time. At least for today.

This is the Year for Me

This year, I resolve to start taking care of myself. Really taking care of myself.

I've tried the new diets; I've sweated through the "no pain, no gain" exercise programs. I've even exorcised my clutter. But this year, I resolve to take care of myself the way I want to be taken care of. I resolve to nurture myself emotionally.

I solemnly pledge that I will not let anyone put me down or walk all over me, and I vow to put my own needs first, at least some of the time. I want to let go of feeding other people's expectations so I can finally learn how to nourish myself and enjoy my life.

This kind of thinking always makes my guilt monster growl. When I hear that snarl in my mind, I start doubting myself, and fretfully fall back into the old, familiar rut of pushing my own needs aside and trying to please everyone else. But this time, I'm determined to get around the guilt monster and change my ways.

I've noticed that I usually feel less guilty about something if I can manage to find out that other people do the same thing. So I did a little research on the web: what kinds of resolutions have other people made?

Here's one: "Part of my New Year's resolution is to become a superhuman, achieving perfection in both mind and body." Wow! And that was only *part* of the resolution! I'm sure that by January 2nd, I'd be wallowing in a stupor of shame and mediocrity, unable to even figure out how to start.

Here's another possibility: The Babylonians, who lived around 2000 BC, had as their most popular resolution a promise to return borrowed farm equipment. Now that's more my style. I can do that! I haven't borrowed any farm equipment!

I've come to the conclusion after years of experience that if I'm going to stick to a resolution, it has to be something simple, something I can commit to with every fiber of my being. I've been pushing myself to do things I don't want to do for so many decades now—and it has never worked!—that the only option left is to try something kinder, gentler, easier. That's the only way I'll be able to start building a history of success. And what's easier than being myself?

So this is the year I resolve to take back my life from the Good-Little-Girl persona that I was trained to hide my real self behind. I don't want to conform any longer. I don't want *People* magazine to tell me who I should emulate. I don't want to listen to the media tell me how I should eat, how much I should weigh, how I should dress, or what I need to change about myself to become a state-of-the-art human being. I want to live life My Way!

I know that the Good Little Girl inside of me is very strong. She's been ruling my life for fifty years, in spite of my occasional escapades into authenticity. She drags me into doing things I don't want to do; she makes me clean when I'd rather be playing. She sets the alarm I have to wake up to. She nags me about keeping up appearances. She makes me smile and nod when I want to get angry or walk away. She spoils my fun by constantly reminding me of the 1,347 things I should be doing instead of enjoying myself, and she doesn't let me have potato chips.

This year, I will have potato chips! I will talk back to the Good Little Girl, and tell her that she can go...do the cleaning herself, because I am going out! I will yell at her if necessary, and tell her in no uncertain terms that I am in charge now. I will ignore the 1,347 things I should be doing while I explore who I Really Am. I will stop worrying about What Other People Think. I resolve to do things my way, and I will not let the Good Little Girl stand in my way, make me talk with people I don't like, eat food I don't want, or buy things that everybody has but that I have no real use for. I'm taking my life back, and she can just go away.

I read somewhere once that we can only give truly from the heart when we've given to ourselves first. That's a theory I'd like to put to the test, though I have to shush the inner voice that says women should always give to others first, and patiently wait their turn. This year, I'm taking my turn, and trusting that when my own heart is full, it will overflow and spill its gifts to the rest of the world.

Flash Fiction

It was a hell of a way to go.

Mahoney's favorite pen, a gold Kimball rollerball with burgundy ink, given to him by his brother-in-law on the fifth anniversary of his first casino opening, poked through the plastic holder in the pocket of his handmade silk shirt, and stabbed him lightly in the chest.

Arsenic swam through his bloodstream—remnants of an old box of rat poison that had fallen into a vat of burgundy ink in the Kimball rollerball plant shortly before Mahoney opened his fourth casino.

The ink spread across his chest as the pen-point entered his skin, and left a huge burgundy stain discovered three hours later by his ex-wife Mavis when she stopped by to inquire about his most recent unpaid alimony debt and found him sprawled in the first-floor half-bath with his pants off and a small solid-gold hoop earring clutched tightly in his left hand.

Schizophrenista Perspectiva,
a.k.a. Monkey Mind

(originally written for the Wergle Flomp poetry contest)

Oh, the human condition!

Stuck in the kitchen,
Moanin' and bitchin',
Corporate power plays,
Cosmic guerilla rays—
Seems like just every day's
Full of BS.
Fulla BS, oh,
Fulla BS.

The wars that we start
Just tear me apart,
Rip a hole in my heart;
And cheese makes me fart!
So I hide in the kitchen,
Moanin' and bitchin',
While Senators increase
Duplicitous palm-grease.
Life is a mess, and it's
Fulla BS!

Fulla BS, yes,
Fulla BS.

Though life is a mess,
I have to confess
That I do love the drama
(That comes from my mama).
And then there's Obama,
Who's full of finesse.

Rub a dub dub,
Three men in a tub—
Oh, aye, there's the rub!
But I gotta eat grub,
So I'm stuck in the kitchen,
Moanin' and bitchin',
Makin' three wishes
'Cause life is a mess.
First I want love,
And then, I want money,
And third is my nose,
Which should stop being runny.
When you call me honey,
I don't think it's funny!
You're fulla BS
—Though it's just a guess
That you're fulla BS.

It's all a disaster
But I can't go faster
I can't seem to master
This strangeness called life.

My job is just shocking
I'm constantly clocking
My time in the focking
Wee-cubicle world.
My talent is hurled
And my salary's squirreled
In somebody's nest...
And yet, I digress.
But nevertheless,
The answer is yes, that
It's fulla BS.
And I must wear a dress.
And *that's* fulla BS, oh,
Fulla BS!
And then there's the press,
Which is FULLA BS!

But I must express
That I'm under duress
From my recent distress
And I can't decompress

So I often regress
And I just can't repress
A relaxed second-guess
That life's fulla BS!
So I hide in the kitchen,
Moanin' and bitchin',
About getting older.
Though I'm getting bolder,
I keep getting colder—
The pain in my shoulder
Just generates stress.

I misplaced that folder....

I'd never suppress
My outlandish success
And I like watercress,
But a day at the mall
Casts a withering pall:
Traffic slows to a crawl
And my mind hits a wall
When my car starts to stall
I can't handle it all!
—Oh, I must make that call...
Can't wait to get home
To hide in the kitchen,
Moaning and bitching

—My eyelid is twitching!
Your phony caresses
And frequent egresses,
Your outright excesses
While Andy obsesses
And Milo oppresses
Will drive me to drink....

....

What did I think?
My brain's on the blink.
There must be a chink
In my gray-matter zinc.
Oh, yes, fulla BS!
It's fulla BS, oh,
Fulla BS—
I must call my shrink.

Google World

As I drive up the slight incline on my way home, I notice the UPS truck sitting at the curb. Must be the books and stuff I ordered. I pull into the driveway, and as I walk up the path I swivel my head towards the truck to wave, but the driver isn't there.

I unlock the side door, and as I push it open, I hear a voice in the kitchen. I can just see him through the doorway from the mud room, leaning against the counter with his cell at his ear, the brown UPS uniform looking like a starched potato sack on his muscular, wiry body.

I throw him a quick salute as I slip out to the living room. A very dark-skinned man turns a piercing gaze my way before he goes back to looking at the collection of paintings on the wall in the hallway. Must be an assistant, learning the ropes.

I grab my remote and log on, googling the pub I plan to stop at later after work, looking for a menu. The wall screen shows a generous bar with beautiful dark wood paneling, the ubiquitous gleam of bottles, and a middle-aged but handsome Irishman with dark hair wiping glasses. Looking for the menu, I click on one link after another. I can't find it. How late are they open? I keep clicking.

The UPS guy is still talking on his cell in the kitchen. I'm getting annoyed—I have to head off to work shortly. I click on another link, and the pub scene morphs out of the wall into a real bar in my living room. But the black-haired Irish guy is gone, so I can't ask him about the menu.

A head pops into the air, like a ghost from a Harry Potter movie. She has black hair and a pretty, pudgy face. I can tell she's Irish from the impish gleam in her eyes. She starts to say something, but I'm in a hurry, so I click another link to get away from her. Startled, she blinks and tries again, opening her mouth a bit wider this time, but I don't want to listen to a pop-up sales pitch, so I click again. Her head jerks back this time as she blinks, and she blows me a loud raspberry as her image fades.

Frustration crawls up my arms; I don't want to be late to work. I click the screen off, and head toward the kitchen to find out what's going on with the UPS guy. He quickly signs off his cell, and hurries over to me as I reach the doorway.

"What's going on?" I ask.

"It was chilly. I had to make a phone call. The back door was unlocked." For some reason, I'm not nervous. I don't know why.

"Fine," I say. "I have to get to work shortly. Where's the package?"

"Over there." He points to the kitchen table, and hands me the bill of lading to sign. I scan it.

"Where's the skirt I ordered?" I ask. It's not on the list.

"They were out," he says. "As I was just saying to my wife, it wouldn't look good on you anyway." He turns to the woman standing behind him, and pulls her over. "This is my wife,

Marietta," he says. I blink at her presence, and nod at her person, and notice the little boy peeking out from behind her skirt. "And this is Joey."

"Hi, Joey," I say. My frustration is growing. It sounds like he'll be hanging out here for awhile, and if I don't leave soon, I'll be late for work.

I turn back into the living room, hoping that if I cut the conversation short, they'll leave now that I've signed for the package. The bar is still there, with a couple of customers sitting on the bar stools, making themselves right at home in my house. The dark-skinned guy is sitting furtively in my Lazy-Boy recliner.

The UPS guy, with his wife and son, follow me back into the living room and sit down. "This is a nice bar," his wife says.

I'm trying to figure out how to be polite as I order all these people out of my house, when a short, fat woman I've never seen before says, "You know what's interesting?" She's sitting in one of those directors' chairs—gold metal with red velvet material. It doesn't belong in my living room.

I start to lower myself on to the sofa, as if I've invited them all over for a chat, but I catch myself, and take the stairs two at a time up to the bathroom so I can collect myself. It's always been the only place where I can shut other people out of my head so I can figure out what to do next.

I pound my fists into the air. "What the hell is this? I have to get to work! How'm I going to get them all out of here?"

I decide I'd better pee before I leave the house, and as I flush, I hear a distant scream that morphs into a mumbled gurgling. I look into the toilet, where bits of hair and pieces of brown fabric twirl downward toward the sewer. Washing my hands, I contemplate the destruction of things and people that were never here in the first place.

I whistle as I descend the stairs to my quiet living room, and grab the remote on my way out, just in case.

Season of the Hunt

Albert and Maggie kept a sharp lookout for prey as they rode the wind past a huge evergreen. Summer had been a tough time: the prey were always scattered, and Albert and Maggie and their kind often weakened and lost many of their friends in the heat of summertime. But now the nights were getting cooler, and once again the smaller prey were gathering into schools during the day.

Albert and Maggie liked the smaller prey better—they were more susceptible, and didn't work so hard at fending off advances. And the fact that the smaller ones gathered into schools made the hunt incredibly easy: one after another, they succumbed to Albert and Maggie, and quickly led them to other prey. But Albert and Maggie also knew that if they could latch on to one of the full-grown humans, they'd be rewarded with a wonderful challenge of a fight.

Albert had gotten an adult human once—and what a thrill!—going for the nose, the throat, the eyes; dividing and dividing until there were millions of Albert-germs all over his prey. The adults made it harder to find new prey, though; they washed their hands a lot, and took some kind of chemical which kept Albert and his offspring from multiplying and spreading to multiply again in another host.

As Albert and Maggie rounded a fat bush, they spied one of the schools nearly below them. It was hard sometimes to navigate the wind; they couldn't always go in exactly the direction they wanted, especially because they were so small. But Maggie made it to the school, smack in the middle of the playground at recess. What luck! Down she dropped into the mouth of a seven-year-old, warm and moist, and Maggie felt right at home. Dividing quickly, she sent newly born Maggies into his nose and throat, and the desired effect was achieved: he sneezed (sending Maggies toward the teacher and two kids in front of him), wiped his nose with his hand, and grabbed the hand of the girl playing next to him.

After school, the Maggies wait silently, gleefully, for the moment their hosts will greet families with warm hugs and sloppy kisses, and gather around the dinner table—providing the Maggies with an opportunity to take over homes, high schools, colleges, and businesses. Occasionally some of the Maggies end up on Kleenex in the toilet; but for today they live in the frenzy and joy of constant reproduction.

For now, Albert and Maggie and their kind rule the world from September to May, year after year. But they live in fear that the humans will invent a new chemical or find that undiscovered herb in the rain forest that will finally add them to the growing list of species that are now extinct on earth, never to return. But for now, there are plenty of tired, stressed-out prey for them to enjoy, and they are happy fulfilling their divine purpose.

Remembrance

The old, gray house at the corner of Third and Main remembered the elderly lady again with fondness. It did not remember much else at all—a few great storms, the day so long ago when a tree root touched its feet and began to grow feeling into it; certainly it didn't remember most of its inhabitants, unimportantly come and gone like ants through its undistinguished efficiencies, but it did remember the old lady.

It did not remember her name, for it didn't know what "name" meant, but it did recall her singing to it (how could it know she might be singing to herself?), and the haunting sound of her tears was impressed forever on its walls.

She had come to the house a young woman with a handsome husband and a life of joy spread out like a platter of sunshine before her. Plans of family and plenty drifted through the rooms and settled in the building's favorite cracks. But the woman's true love went off one day, with teary parting—the building heard "in uniform"—and had never returned.

The building watched, for months, for years, and felt the woman dry and shrivel. It tried to comfort her; it felt her sadness and despair, but could do nothing for her but enclose her, keep her warm and safe.

One recent day, the house had felt the woman's presence leaving. And, puzzled, it felt her rooms: the air she had breathed, the floors she'd walked, the windows she'd looked out of, but it sensed an unfamiliar something new: the cracks of love which joy had fallen into were being filled by men with trowels and plaster; her floors and walls were covered now with paint and carpet; and her smell, the smell of life itself, was dying. The building couldn't breathe as well with cracks filled up and coated walls, and it missed the ebb and flow of life within her rooms.

The old, gray house still sits at the corner of Third and Main, fondly remembering, searching its walls each day for the presence of its beloved.

My Old Dreams by the Ancient Road

Some gnarled old tree
That stands at the side of an ancient road
Seems to speak my life with its branches,
Holding me and my dreams in its twisted, strong arms
Each withered knot
Is a fantasy unrealized
Its peeling bark,
My hopes unraveling.

Its largest branch
Undressed by leaves, and barren,
Points down the ancient road,
And urges me to travel
Past this tree that knows my history.

And as the road unfolds
And leaves the dusty memories behind
I see green meadows spreading
Out beyond the ending of the road
A pasture of new possibilities,
A grove of young and as yet unmarked trees
Where I may wander
And again create my hopes and dreams anew

So they may bloom beyond the gnarled tree
That held my old dreams by the ancient road.

I Am From...

(Response to a writing prompt based on a poem
by George Ella Lyon)

I am from retracted Easter eggs
From china reminiscences of grieving
From cracked inheritances, perfect public images
The muddy bottom of the pond obscured
By twinkling on the surface.

I am from a tiger butterfly,
A saint beneath a burlap bag
The noise of dirty, overcrowded streets
And deepness of a library
From Jeroldine and William, the dancer and the priest.

I am from an ever-growing hunger
From lust for life and famished exploration
From glittering possibilities caged in tiny, airless boxes
Of rules and regulations and the way it has to be.

I am from the vision of the eagle
The animal who senses all
And acts from total instinct

I am from the stars and earth
From places where what's truth is understood.

Pardon

Pardon the interruption...

But things are not going at all the way I planned. It's upsetting. I thought ahead, I carefully charted the route, and I think I've stayed on the road I started out on, but somehow it changed, and for the last several years I've been driving through a swamp, ducking the branches flying at me and trying to cover my head so I don't get pooped on by one of the vultures that seem to be constantly flying over since I got off track.

Pardon the interruption...

...but wasn't being a grownup supposed to mean that you got to do things your own way, that you knew how to get what you wanted, like my mother did, and that other people always respected you, just because you were a grownup?

Pardon the interruption...

...but we're having a really hard time down here. And pardon my saying so, but weren't you supposed to help us, to keep us safe from harm, to show us the way to heaven?

Pardon the interruption...

...but who are all those people that have no respect for others, that dump all their feelings on other people, that demand bigger bonuses from their companies when other people are starving? Are they really human, or did they get suckered in by what's-his-name down below like it says in the Big Book?

Pardon the interruption...

...but I think I'm really lost. Could you say, "Let there be light" again so I can see my way through the swamp? I could really use a hand here...

Careful!

I first learned to pet kitties when I was two. My mother taught me, because she caught me pulling their tails.

"Gently, gently," she said, taking my hand and smoothing it down the kitty's body from head to tail.

I practiced on numerous kitties over the years: Muffin, Francis, Punkin, Princess, Midnight, Skippy, and Emma—and the one thing I know for sure is that every kitty likes to be petted differently.

My mother never discovered that nugget of wisdom. She liked everything done her way, with no allowances for individual preferences. But each kitty has its own style, just like each human does.

Muffin loved to be scratched, and purred most happily when I rubbed her head firmly, pushing her ears back and forth, even flattening them so she looked like a bunny.

Francis really liked it when I stroked his lovely white-and-yellow tummy very slowly, or when I smoothed the fur under his chin over and over. His eyes would light with joy before they closed in blissful sleep. Princess was very elegant, and liked very gentle petting. She would lift her head and smile as I stroked her soft fur.

Emma likes gentle, short pats, ending in my fingers pulling her ears slowly away from her head. She only likes her chin scratched once in awhile—and she lets me know when by jutting her jaw into my hand. She absolutely does not like her tummy touched. At all. Ever.

"All cats like their tummies rubbed," my mother said one day when my parents were visiting me in New York.

"Try that with Emma, and you might as well be giving blood," I said as I gently pulled one of Emma's contented ears. My mother snorted and reached out to prove her statement.

At least it was a short trip to the hospital.

The Woods

I loved to go to the woods when I was small. The woods were real—the trees didn't lie, and the soft green moss that nestled in their roots was more inviting and comforting than the bargain-basement sheets I slept on at home.

I loved to walk in the woods because I knew what to expect there. At home, God was always popping out from somewhere to scare the life out of me. God was my brother, somehow knowing when I was on my way to the bathroom, hiding behind the door in the dark, and jumping out at me like a savage jack-in-the-box; and my mother, who I was always afraid of anyway, banging pots and pans around in the kitchen while she said, "I'm not angry!" in an angry voice; and my father—a gentle, submissive, compassionate man who turned into a monster when he punished my brother for every little imperfection. God was everywhere when I was growing up, watching and counting each little mistake.

We went to church every Sunday, and always on holidays. There I learned all about God and his terrible swift sword, and all the rules I needed to follow. People at church talked a lot about God, and said they were doing a lot of things for God, but I couldn't find God there myself. I thought perhaps I just didn't understand the rules. I liked the woods better, because I could remember the rules of the woods, and they weren't hard to live by.

My parents worked hard to teach us the important lessons of life: give to others before giving to yourself; make sure you rack up plenty of points so you get into heaven; always follow the rules, even if they might be wrong; and don't ever enjoy anything, because that's a sin. They didn't build character—they built a robot.

Many times throughout my life I've wondered where God is. When I needed a helping hand, or someone else did, or yet another war began, I looked for God, in vain.

Now I'm in the middle of my life. I live near the woods again, and I go for walks there, sometimes on Sunday mornings when other people go to church. And I've discovered that God is everywhere in the woods, but only in a few churches. I find God in the woods—in the wind as it caresses my hair and makes the tree branches dance, in the sun that warms my skin and makes the birds sing, and in the plants themselves, which somehow know that if they keep growing, they'll create a beautiful plant or tree from a tiny little seed.

And I find God in my good friends, who offer help when I ask for it, and appreciate the help I give them—and I don't keep track of the heaven points anymore.

And best of all, I've found God in my heart, where She always was.

Not Quite Me, Not Quite You

Do you ever wake up in the middle of the night, in your own home, and suddenly, it's not familiar? You know what it looks like—there's the bed, that's my dresser, those are the two windows that look out on the front lawn—but you don't feel like it's yours, it's somebody else's.

I used to think it meant I had fallen into some deep form of the Power of Now, as if I was so steeped in this moment of reality that all of my memories—my deepest sense of who I was and how I'd lived—had died away into an existential nothingness.

In the middle of the night sometimes, you feel your life around you.

Sometimes you're glad you're there.

Sometimes you wish for more.

Who are we really? An inimitable collection of thoughts, desires, feelings, and behaviors, arising from the clear, true impulses of the soul and oozing up through the primordial brainstem to get trapped and muddled in the miasmic web of childhood indoctrination?

My pen sears the paper as I try to scribble away the scars of my childhood.

When I was small, my parents criticized me endlessly:

"Get your elbows off the table!"

"Don't talk with your mouth full."

"Change your clothes. That looks trashy."

"Pull in your tummy!"

Parts of me went away when it happened, so there have always been blank spaces in who I am, even while I continued to function: to love, to eat, to work, to play. Parts of me were always somewhere else.

But lately, they've been coming back at 4 a.m.

dis·so·ci·á·tion: In psychiatry, a defense mechanism in which specific, anxiety-provoking thoughts, emotions, or physical sensations are separated from the rest of the psyche. Also, the process by which a compound body breaks up into simpler constituents.

What happens to those parts we leave behind? Do they swim, untethered, in the deepest layers of our cells, drifting in the sea of consciousness, bewildered molecules of who we were and who we're meant to be, waiting for their chance to come alive?

I am angry today. I don't know why. Nothing has happened to produce my mood.

It's one of them—the unlived selves, a fragment lost in time and space because there was no room for it to grow. It wants out; it wants to tell me what it needs and how it felt and where it wants to go. It wants to shout its fury. It wants to live, to move my limbs and make my choices, to be a part of who I am becoming.

It wants me; it wants to *be* me. Like my mother did.

What happened to the infant me, that pure, sweet breath of bright new life who knew no pain, who lay there crying, lonely, while Mommy cleaned the kitchen?

Is she this me who wakes at 4 a.m. and doesn't recognize my life?

I reach out my hand, and welcome her into my heart.

At school, I hid behind my glasses, pretending I knew what the world was all about. The memories of fists and belts hid deep inside where I hoped no one could see them. And then one day, I put the memories so far away I didn't see them anymore myself.

So many parts of me got left behind. But they're still living somewhere deep inside, waiting for their turns.

Someday, if I wake up in the middle of the night often enough, all of me will be here.

My Mother Lives in the Can Opener

For most of my adult life, I've struggled with a fear of success. Though I've accomplished a number of my goals, over time I've discovered that I often resist accomplishing almost as much as I strive for it.

When I was small, my mother didn't seem to want me to succeed. I'm sure that if I'd asked her, she would have said that she did, but instead of encouraging my efforts and praising my successes, she belittled my attempts to achieve and criticized my skills. Nothing was ever good enough, and when I did grab a wee bit of limelight or attain a long-cherished goal, she stepped into the midst of my glory and collected most of the attention for herself.

I know that my mother's own childhood experience weighed heavily on her psyche. She was the youngest of three daughters, and her mother dressed the two older girls alike. My grandmother told my mother that since the family already had two girls, she should have been a boy.

She was even named for her father, Jerold. All her life, my mother listened to people misspell her name "Geraldine," and had to correct them by saying, "No, it's J-e-r-o-l-dine." She also grew up in a time and place where women weren't expected to work outside the home, so most of her activities outside the family consisted of involvement in church programs. She didn't have much room to grow and explore, and never learned how to nourish herself. Though she was a very strong woman, she always seemed to need others to hold her up. Mostly me.

As I grew from a child into a woman in the midst of the women's lib movement, my mother became even needier. Whenever I told her about something new I was exploring, or a new job, a new possibility, a new friend, she quickly turned the conversation back to herself and her activities in the small town where my parents lived.

Over the years, I began to understand that her behavior generated in me a feeling of being "yanked around." Just as soon as I began to feel sure-footed on a path, she would "yank" me in some other direction, needing me to give more attention to her and her activities. I wrote about my quest to recover from this pattern in my memoir, *The Box of Daughter*.

After almost 50 years of being yanked around whenever the mood hit my mother, subconsciously I began to equate being successful with getting jerked around. It took me a long time to figure that one out. At the time of my mother's passing, I breathed a sigh of relief. Though I loved her, the pull of her needs had consistently thrown me off balance, and I never truly found my "legs" in life. I thought that once she was gone, it would be much easier for me to find my way. I thought my fear of success would disappear.

But the psyche has a tendency to keep repeating whatever pattern we're used to. Even when I felt my life was running relatively smoothly, that constant fear of being yanked around again ran amok under the surface of my thoughts. And sometimes life does throw a curve ball—each one triggered my old fear that even if I could really accomplish the goals I set for myself, somehow I would get yanked off course again (or the other shoe was going to drop).

I have an electric can opener that works perfectly about 75% of the time. The rest of the time, it tears the paper on the can and gets stuck, or it won't turn the can 'round at all. This can opener always triggers those old feelings of being jerked around because I never know when it will misbehave, and it's almost a surprise when it works well.

I thought of tossing it and using a hand-held opener, since I don't open cans very often (mostly for my cat), but when I realized that it reminded me of my mother, I decided to keep it, and assign it the duty of carrying the entirety of this old pattern so I didn't have to worry about being jerked around in the other aspects of my life. So far it's doing its job pretty well.

I'm sure that life will still throw me curve balls, but knowing that my mother lives only in the can opener makes it much easier for me to visualize, work toward, and create success, no matter how small the steps I take.

Oyster Girl

One tiny grain of sand
Slips into the oyster's shell—
The pearl is born.

One criticism suggesting inadequacy
Taken into a young girl's heart
Opens the wound.

One moment of that hurt which cuts too deep
Begins construction of the shell
Which grows too fast.

Amid the daily criticisms and injustices,
The lack of proffered love and self-respect
Hardens the shell
Into a lifelong barricade.

Where Does the Phone Live?

When I was a kid, I wondered about life. How did adults always know exactly what to do in every situation? It seemed like the point of growing up was to learn enough about things and to get sure enough of yourself that everything would always be in perfect order, and nothing would ever throw you off your stride. I thought feelings just sort of disappeared when you reached adulthood, because none of the adults I knew ever seemed to have any.

I figured that I'd be learning all about life in school, and that they had it set up so that you'd learned everything you needed to know about life by the time you graduated from high school. Then you were ready for the world, and you could drive, and get a job, and live happily ever after in adulthood.

But I only thought that because there weren't any problems in our family. Oh, no! And nothing ever went wrong. We did everything perfectly, and always knew exactly what we were doing in every situation.

Except for me, of course. I never knew what I was doing in any situation. I could mess up a perfectly ordered silverware drawer in five seconds just by looking for a spatula. And I put everything in the wrong places. "But wait," I'd think to myself, "I'm sure that notepad was right next to the phone when I picked it up," even though my mother assured me, "No, it belongs under the phone." I never saw it under the phone.

Those are the kinds of things I thought adulthood would clear up. But it didn't. In fact, during many of the 347 visits I made to my mother's house as an adult, that notepad lived in at least 16 different spatial relationships with the phone. In fact, the phone itself moved around, too, and apparently, according to my mother, I never did find the proper place to put it back after I used it.

I always thought as a kid that going to college gave you a special veneer, sort of like a protective shell, so that nobody could argue with you. But mine never grew, even though I graduated many years ago. I know it never grew because my mother still argues with me, mostly about the phone and its significant-other notepad.

Of course, I majored in theater in college, so that probably explains why I didn't learn how to make perfect choices in every situation like my mother does. And according to my mother, I probably never will. And just in case, I keep my notepad as far away from the phone as I can get it.

The Great Discovery

Right now, my life feels like 90% stupidity. Get up, fix food, wash dishes, go to work, come home, fix food, wash dishes, go to bed. So many parts of life to try to keep together, and most of them I don't even want to do. Do they live like this in Tibet?

I always imagine they do everything more spiritually in Tibet. So it must be that I haven't yet made The Great Discovery that will Change My Life Forever. Is it just screened from view right now, or do I have to change somehow in order to make The Great Discovery? And what is it anyway? Will I know it when I see it?

Saturday morning: I'm getting up today with the goal of finding replacements for all of the parts of my life that don't work, like replacing the parts of a machine that have worn out or stopped working. I start out with the usual get up, fix food, wash dishes, and then....

Suddenly I'm faced with a strange, empty hole. "What should I replace first?" I ask my heart. The answer comes: Anger in a nutshell. I think that's right—there has been so much anger floating around in my system about how my life is 90% stupidity that there's not much room for anything else. "What should I replace my anger with?" I ask my inner child. "Fun!" she says. I ponder this as I switch on the TV to look for something fun.

They've interrupted the TV broadcast to let us know there's been an earthquake in Tibet. Have I finally made The Great Discovery?

A Clean Slate

The Time is Now. Sometimes life offers the chance to clean your plate, to start with a clean slate. The problem is that, at a time like this, the tendency is to intellectualize. That's my problem: do I want to do this? Or that? Which direction should I be moving in now? I always thought I wanted to do this other thing, but I'm a different person now—do I still want to do that?

My brain gets so full of ideas and possibilities and what-if's that my body gets frozen, unable to actualize anything.

What I need is someone like Star Trek's android Data to tell me how to clear my neural net and set up new filters for incoming information so I don't get so overwhelmed by the infinite possibilities before me. And if I was like Data, I wouldn't have to feel. That would save an incredibly large amount of time, which I could then spend ruminating over more ideas and possibilities.

Maybe that's the problem: too many feelings. When I intellectualize about what to do with my clean slate, all these fears and uncertainties and doubts come up: what if I choose the wrong path? What if I choose the right one, and then I discover I can't do it or it leads somewhere other than where I thought it was going to go? And the most frightening question of all: What if I'm actually successful this time? What the heck do I do then?

Data, I need you!

Peas in a Pod

(from *The Box of Daughter: Healing the Authentic Self*)

My mother is at it again.

"Have some sauerkraut."

"No, thank you." I've told her at least 237 times that I don't like sauerkraut.

"Just have a little."

My jaw tenses, my hands want to fist up. I know where this is headed. "No, I don't like it."

"Well, I do," she says loudly, as if that should make me like it.

"Well, I don't."

She pushes the dish over so it tings the edge of my plate. "Try some. You might change your mind."

I feel like my castle door is being charged over and over by a battering ram. But I still have to be polite. If I show signs of anger, she'll exact revenge in untold ways. "No, thank you. I've tried it. I don't like it." By now, all of my muscles are tense with the need to shout, "Leave me alone!" But I don't.

"You don't know what you're missing," she replies.

Yes, I do, I think to myself. I know what sauerkraut tastes like. But I don't say anything. She has to have the last word. It's one of the unwritten rules in our house.

She ignores me for the rest of the meal. When I try to make up for not liking sauerkraut by asking her if she'd like help with the dishes, she snarls and turns her back on me.

"No! You just go have fun, do whatever you want, I don't care!"

The familiar feeling of my stomach landing on the ground assails me again.

My mother's Borderline Personality Disorder steamrolls me into a corner where there is no escape. As a BPD sufferer, she has no real sense of self, so she tries to create one by getting everyone else to mirror her own preferences.

"Are you sure you want chicken? *I'm* having shrimp."

"Long hair is harder to take care of. That's why I keep mine short."

"I guess you can wear pants, but *I'm* going to wear a dress."

"Why are you reading *that*? Now, here's a good book...."

The bathroom is my only refuge. I go there when I need to create a boundary for myself. It's the only place I can feel myself and hear my own thoughts. Without that border of walls, of civilization's blessed convention providing privacy from another's intrusiveness, I do not exist. My thoughts, my feelings, my beliefs have been since birth only a reflection of my mother, grounded in her bizarre and unwavering self-focus.

We're shopping for school supplies.

"You need a new notebook," my mother says. "Pick one out."

I look at the notebooks with their red, yellow, blue, and purple covers. I wait for my mother to make a suggestion, but she's quiet, so I seem to have a choice this time. I choose the purple one. Purple is my favorite color.

"How about the red one?" my mother suggests, as I pull out the purple one.

"I like purple better. It's my favorite color."

"You never told me that," she says, even though I have. "The red one looks better."

I have a choice between getting the color I want and being snubbed for the rest of the day, or taking the red one, making her happy, and feeling a bit sad every time I look at it. The need for peace wins out today, and I take the red one. I feel some of her dissatisfaction with her life leap over and land on me. Some of my confidence jumps over to her.

For the rest of the year, whenever I use the red notebook, I think of my mother, and wish I had picked the purple one.

My mother exerted continuous effort to make us both alike. She wanted us to be identical because she had been the third wheel in her childhood, the one her two sisters left out in the cold.

"You're an ice cream lover, just like me," she blurted one night as I scooped ice cream into a dish.

Getting dinner ready, she took a can of olives from the cabinet. "We both like olives." After a big meal: "You have a tummy, like mine."

Washing dishes together, "Like mother, like daughter."

When I put on my favorite skirt, "You look better in A-line skirts." That's what she wore.

And out of nowhere, "We're like two peas in a pod."

When I did something she liked: "That's MY daughter!" When I did what I wanted, she ignored me, or criticized me: "That's not right. Do it this way. No, that's not the way. Here, try this instead. No, you're not doing it right. Well, never mind, just let me do it."

My mother never wanted to know who I was. She only wanted me to be exactly like her, to want what she wanted. In public and at home, I was always "Jerry's daughter," as if I were only an extension of her, and not a person in my own right. "Doesn't Jerry's daughter play the piano nicely?" people would say. "Oh, look, there's Jerry's daughter." And I always felt like an extension, too, as if I wasn't a real person, but only an appendage of my mother, to be put on or taken off at will. Even though I struggled persistently to become my own person, to create a comfortable distance between us, I remained an appendage, in both of our minds, for as long as she lived.

By the time I was a teenager, I had forgotten how to think. I just went along with whatever anyone else wanted. If anyone asked me what I liked or what I wanted to do, I said, "I don't know." I didn't know how to make decisions; I didn't even know

I had choices. The world was programmed for me by my mother's whims, and I just went along with it. Time after time, I hid parts of myself in the walls of my inner void, until all that was left was the polite me, and it ruled my life for many years. The real me hid at the bottom of the void, waiting for my turn.

When I was twenty, I decided that I never wanted to be like my mother. I was more comfortable being gentle, respectful, and cooperative, like my father. But decades later, after her death, I realized that in making that choice, I had left behind my strength, my power, and my intensity—my passion for life. And I discovered then that underneath all of the pain and anger and frustration that I had carried throughout the life of our relationship, I had loved my mother fiercely: her intensity, her vivacity, her dynamic hunger for excitement and experience. Many times, she was the life of the party. She fought her demons to the best of her ability, and tried to live a good and moral life. She was tremendously creative, had incredible energy, and was always coming up with new ideas. She grabbed life with both hands and gobbled it up, and then she went looking for more.

Throughout my life, I lived in constant fear of my mother's retribution, and continuous awareness of the profound anguish she held inside, which I finally learned in midlife was a result of her struggle with Borderline Personality Disorder. Though I toiled endlessly in my attempts to make everything better, the chaos, her anguish, and my sense of myself as a failure persisted. We had no real emotional connection, and I felt absolutely alone. When I looked inside of myself, there was only an endless void. I knew *I* was in there, because I saw things, and I had thoughts, and I could see out. But there was nothing else inside of me, no link to other people or the outside world that I could hold on to. All that was left inside was a solid and absolute feeling of worthlessness and insignificance.

And in spite of being afraid of her, I wanted her love so very much, I knew I would keep trying to get it as long and as hard as I could.

How to Make Monkey Mind Work for You

I grew up in what I like to call The Box of Daughter: a rigid structure of rules about values, beliefs, thinking, feeling, and behaving, set forth for me by super-religious parents who grew up in boxes of their own. For a large part of my life, my thinking bounced around within the confines of that box— worrying the old worries, thinking the old thoughts, feeling the old pain, and acting out pretty much the same compulsions time after time—stuck in ever-repeating loops of Monkey Mind.

I've always loved reading about quantum physics, and marveling at the infinite possibilities in the universe. But I couldn't seem to get many of those wonderful possibilities to happen in my life because I was stuck in that old structure, with the childhood voices bulldozing their doubts, fears, and negative mumblings right over what I was trying to create. As I've endeavored over the years to deepen and expand my spirituality, I've connected more and more with the Divine Creative Force, the constant, growth-oriented creative energy of Life. "This is how I'm meant to live," I would think, and then I'd go right back to Monkey Mind.

I've come to believe that there must be a purpose for Monkey Mind—that Nature intended for us to do something with it, that it's not simply an aberration that evolved in us as life got more complicated. One night in the bathtub (which is where I do my best creative thinking), I noticed a correlation between the constant flow of creative energy in the Universe and Monkey Mind, which is a also constant flow of energy—but in my case, energy that's ricocheting off the inside walls of the mental box I grew up in.

A hypothesis bloomed in my mind that Monkey Mind might be a twisted form of what Nature originally intended to be constant Creative Thought. My mind turned to one of my favorite pastimes, puttering. When I'm puttering, my mind often flows from one thing to another, seemingly at random, and I usually feel like I'm smack in the now—dealing with one task, then another, in any order I choose to. It may not necessarily be truly creative, but there is a forward flow that I don't experience with Monkey Mind.

When I'm in Monkey Mind, there are usually only a few selected thoughts going through my mind, circling around and around, bumping up against each other in their rush to be first. There's no forward movement. I suppose it's a form of creativity; however, I'm a little fearful of what I create when I'm in Monkey Mind.

I've been tinkering with different possibilities for manifesting what I want in my life, and that's led me to discover a way to get out of Monkey Mind and into Creative Mind, which not only brings me right into the Now, but opens my mind to more and more and more possibilities. It's sort of like the same type of circling thought, but it never returns to the starting place on the circle. The thoughts do not repeat themselves—they curve around from one possibility to the next, to another idea, another way, another dream....

When I'm working on a task that I hope will encourage something I want to manifest, if I let my creative mind jump from possibility to possibility ("...and then what? And then what happens? And what else?"), I'm able to keep jumping over that little doubting voice that used to create most of my reality ("...it's not happening, it's not going to happen, it won't happen.") As long as I stay in that creative mind, jumping from one possibility to the next like the image I have of a fractal (winding out into more designs and spirals of possibility), that little doubting voice doesn't have a chance to interject its repetitive thoughts. As long as I don't go back to square one, Monkey Mind doesn't get me.

I'm sure the Divine Creative Force is out there saying to itself, "And what else can I create? What does this make me think of? And what other possibilities might there be?" That's how I think Nature intended us to use Monkey Mind. I can't imagine It thinking, "Wait, I have to go back and check that flower...Whoops, that tree isn't quite tall enough...Maybe I shouldn't have created that volcano..."

Creative Mind is similar to the way I remember thinking as a child: "Why do bumblebees buzz? What do they feel like? Ouch!!" But once we get into school, we're essentially trained to think in Monkey Mind: reciting facts over and over to commit them to memory, learning the rules of English and using them every time we write (even when we're writing creatively), and even sometimes having our physical play at recess structured into games full of rigid rules.

It's no wonder we learn to think in circles (or in my case, squares) instead of fractally. We learn how to do Monkey Mind in school, just like we learn how to do everything else.

So here are a few tips for getting out of Monkey Mind and learning what Creative Mind might feel like inside your head:

1. When doing a repetitive task like washing the dishes, try enumerating to yourself in your mind every step that you're taking, and start inserting new thoughts: "Putting soap on the sponge, rinsing the plate, I wonder who made this plate, rubbing the sponge in a circular motion, and could I rub it the other direction? I wonder what country this sponge was made in, and how are sponges made anyway?" Keep pushing yourself to come up with new thoughts. Don't let old familiar ones edge their way in.

2. When you're making efforts to manifest something in your life, don't stop with the first picture you get. Keep expanding it: "And then what? And what would that mean? And what could I do with that?" Draw other things into the visualization or energy output that aren't necessarily related in order to keep expanding your vision: "And maybe a surprise would happen, and my health could be better, and I might live somewhere else..."

I find when I'm trying to manifest that if I try to hold a particular vision for very long, that little doubter elbows its way in and starts telling me how it's not going to happen. That's because trying to hold the vision means I'm <u>fixating</u>—same thing as my Monkey Mind going around in a circle. I have to keep changing the vision slightly (preferably <u>growing</u> it) in order to stop fixating, and that prevents the Doubter from getting a handhold.

3. Go for a walk and talk silently to yourself about what you see: "That tree's a little crooked. It's taller than the others. I saw a bird go by—wonder what kind it is? Sure are a lot of weeds here. I wouldn't be driving that fast on this curvy road. I can feel my knees every time I take a step..." Keep your focus moving, so it doesn't settle inside your mind. Getting into your body is a great way to get into the Now.

4. When you've got the feeling, try it with creating: "How would I change that tree so I'd like it better? Can I walk more gently so my knees don't hurt? If I could change the color of the sky for one day, what would I change it to? What would I put there if there wasn't a sky?"

Ever notice how, when children are creating, they say, "And then....And then....And then..."? That's Creative Mind: coming up with another possibility, another idea, another option, another dream, like constant brainstorming. It's a little tiring the first few times you get into it, but it "uses up" that Monkey Mind energy so you can rest afterwards. It does take practice. But I believe from the bottom of my heart that it puts us into powerful alignment with the Divine Creative Force.

It's so much easier to keep the mind moving along a creative path than it is to try and shut out negative thoughts.

Who knows what you'll come up with? See if you can get into Creative Mind, and you won't have to not think about that elephant that's not in the room.

Heaven and Hell

I think somebody came up with the idea of heaven so many years ago to keep us all putting one foot in front of the other in spite of the pain, the angst, the total tooth-clenching, gut-wrenching frustration of living a human life.

What they should do is give us a little vacations in heaven now and then, where we can bounce lots of checks and eat all the junk food we want, and where those niggling physical problems disappear for the duration.

That would make it much easier to jump back into the fray.

Or, if there was a criminal who refused to reform, or—YES! a corrupt politician or CEO of a major corporation who embezzled funds or treated employees in a disgraceful way, we could send them on a Holiday to Hell where they would be forced to change their ways or be damned for eternity.

Somewhere...

Money doesn't grow on trees—at least in America. But so many new herbs and amazing cures for diseases have been found in various rainforests that it makes me wonder if there might be a couple of money trees way back in there, spewing out dollars and just waiting for the Federal Reserve Board to show up with a special vacuum and suck them all up.

Helpless Sunshine

The sun doesn't have any choice, you know. Plants use its energy to grow, and it can't stop them. Up and down, up and down, round and round and round, day after day, human lifetime after human lifetime. At least I'm not the only one who seems to go in circles forever.

But, yes—now I remember—the Sun stays right where it is, and *we* go around *it*. So it really is helpless—just *stuck* there, in one place, forever and ever. I know how that feels, too. We're going round and round, forever and ever, in a slightly elliptical dance out in the void between the stars and comets and lumps of plastic bottles that coalesce in the darkness of space.

Miles away
In the cold, dark deadness of space
The sun spews its hot light
Into the dark corners of creation
Warming the sad planet
Where humanity lives and dies.

Powerless Snow

Snow has no choice—it just falls from the sky whether it wants to or not. If clouds decide to provide the right conditions, snow gets created. It can't even procreate. If the ground is cold, and there's not too much sun, it gets to stay alive until spring. If the air is warm, it dies into water or dissolves into air before it even hits the ground.

People shove it into huge chunks to get if off their driveways. Kids cut it with sled runners when it has landed on a hill. Is it nice, or horrible, to be all clumped up with other snow in a snowball or snowperson?

Snow clumps
Always cold
To warm itself, to sit in front of a winter's fire means
certain death—
Or absolute freedom, as the rivulets of water run down my
boots
And puddle in joy at my feet.

Artifact

Artifact. What a strange word, like a blend of "artist" and "fact." Does art only become a fact when it's old and dirty? Or when they clean it up? Heads, busts, horns, figures, arrowheads, broken plates, Volkswagens...

Maybe the word "artifact" only describes something that has outgrown its usefulness, like the government, or the war, or last week's tuna salad, pushed to the back of the fridge.

Random Thoughts

—Winter is the time when I begin to get a sense of just how deep I go.

—Once found, the self can never be lost. It is the finding in which we must lose ourselves.

—There will always be enough negative experiences. So we should enjoy the positive ones as intensely as we can.

—Was playing with dolls supposed to be the way to learn how to be independent and make choices for ourselves? Or a way to live vicariously through the dolls, because we weren't allowed to?

—Each person grows up learning that they'll get only a certain percentage of what they want, depending on their family situation. Mine was about 3-5%. It's a relief knowing that the percentage can change radically in adulthood if we want it to.

Where We Are Now

The world before fire was cold and dark. People huddled in their caves, except when they went out to hunt and gather, and at night they lived by smell and sense of touch. Survival was the keynote—every minute, every day.

Man searched for meaning in nature's moon and stars, her plants and animals and seasons.

Nature was in charge then. If she chose a colder winter, men died. If her predator children were hungry enough, a clan's population could be reduced by half in the darkest moment of the night.

When man found fire, he began to control Nature. He could turn her light and heat on and off at will, he could roast her children and fatten up the clan so more of them survived the winter.

And when man had gained this small amount of control over Nature, he became dissatisfied that he did not control every aspect of her. He began using her plants and trees to build dwellings, and collecting her water to make her food grow better and faster. Nature became something to *use*; no longer protector and provider, no longer a being in her own right.

Now man, like God, can say, "Let there be light," and flip a light switch on. He can bring the heat of fire to his home by turning a dial. But the real fire—the fire within that drives man to create, to love, to explore—has grown dimmer since that first grasping for control of Nature.

Nature struggles for control in the only way she can: by trying to throw man off of her body with earthquakes, trying to drown him in floods. But still he persists, and he calls her desperate attempts to regain control "dangerous." But She is only asking to have the control of her body returned to her.

Without the inner fire, man has lost his connection to Nature. He created clocks and calendars and computers to help him in his search for meaning and fulfillment. But now the clocks and calendars and computers control man and his world. He gave up his inner fire, wrested control of the earth from Nature, and gave control to inanimate objects. Now he believes that objects are where his inner fire comes from.

Shopaholism and Creativity

When man first began to evolve, if he needed something, he had to create it—clothing, hunting gear, shelter. He couldn't just go out and buy it, he had to figure out how to make it and then use his own two hands to gather materials and put it together. Now all we have to do is go to the nearest mall, turn on the computer, or, if we're actually making it ourselves, buy a book and follow the step-by-step instructions.

What if the need to shop, to acquire new clothes and gadgets and decorative items for our living spaces, is not really based on a desire to *have* things, but is rather a twisted variation of the basic human need to create? The creative drive can be stifled by a dull and repetitive job, relationship, life. We want *new things*—yet how quickly the enjoyment of a new dress or gadget wears off, leaving us with a recurring desire for something else that's new.

Shopping offers an outlet for creativity: we get to make choices based on color, design, size, function. But instead of putting those choices together into new and innovative forms, we just pick a thing that includes all of our choices. Of course, if our day-to-day needs can be so easily met—without hours, days, or weeks of creating what we need to survive—we are much more free to create whatever and however we want. But because creating can be a difficult and frustrating process, most people tend to back away from it and take the easy way out, which is to go and buy something new. Then we feel as if we've created something, with none of the frustration and effort.

So the next time you feel the urge to go out and get a new dress or the latest gadget, try taking just a moment to create something first: get a Flair and make patterns on paper (doesn't matter if you can't draw!), write a poem (nobody will ever see it if you don't want them to), or make up a new song in the shower. You might just become a createaholic. And who knows what great idea you might come up with next?

A Time to Rejoice

The world has been looking pretty bad over the last couple of decades. Executives in charge of our biggest, most powerful companies have been found with both hands in the corporate till, cheating not only their employees and companies, but Uncle Sam as well. And the Catholic Church has been forced to uncover the dirty underwear that has been moldering at the bottom of its laundry hamper for many years.

My first impulse in responding to these situations comes from habit: as I wash the dishes and do my chores, I shake my head and say to myself, "How can any human being do those things? The world just isn't like it used to be!" (and I'm only 45).

But underneath my old habit of viewing events like these in a negative way blooms a small flower of hope: I realize that the exposing of these indignities simply means that the light of truth is beginning to shine, in some ways for the first time, into the dark and dirty corners of our corporate and religious worlds.

For centuries, the church has been held in the highest esteem. Like the kings of old England, it sat at God's right hand, bringing down spiritual rules for us to live by, declaring itself the foremost interpreter of God's words. Its leaders could do no wrong, but could always point out when others did. And though throughout much of this century the aim of most companies was to Satisfy the Customer, now major corporations have grown so huge that the human heart has become separated from the spiritual act of work, and who cares if the customer is satisfied as long as those in charge make a Big Profit?

What I tend to forget is that these events didn't happen yesterday, or last week, or last month—they've been happening for years, under the surface, like plants growing dark and slimy roots while the flower above the ground remains nearly lily-white.

This realization changes my perspective: I no longer see these events as evidence that our world is quickly deteriorating; rather I see that the haze of deceit is lifting, and these disorders are being brought to light so that the world can be healed. As I think about it, I much prefer the perspective which suggests that the world is changed for the better, even in a small way, by the clarity that comes when a young boy shouts, "But the Emperor is wearing no clothes!" over the perspective that simply turns its back and pretends not to notice.

We're offered a choice as to how we can view these events, and if we believe the words of spiritual sages over the centuries, then right now, at this moment in time, we have the chance to recreate the world with our thoughts. We can either moan and complain about how terrible the world has become, and thus create a world in which ever more inhumane and blasphemous events occur, or we can see these revelations of inexcusable behavior as an attempt by our Collective Consciousness to clear out the manure, wash the muck from the windows, weed the garden so that we can start over and plant the seeds for a new world of our own choosing—a world of peace and light and harmony.

It seems as if our world is crumbling, piece by piece, into a pile of dirty secrets and unconscionable lies. And yet what's really happening is that the old, rotted structure is tumbling, making room for us to build what we want in its place. Together we can raise the phoenix from the ashes and make the world what we want it to be.

The world is beginning to heal. It's a time to rejoice.

Grow Your Own Economy

It's looking pretty bleak out there—job loss, lower corporate profits, sagging economy—and we're recreating it all over again right now as we focus on it. If quantum physicists are correct, as we each contribute our thoughts to the collective reality, we're creating exactly what we're afraid of.

It's not that we're particularly to blame. It's pretty difficult to focus on small positive events when the media thrusts every negative possibility into our eyes and ears whenever we tune in to what's happening in the world around us. But collectively, every time we focus on news we don't really even want to hear, we are manifesting our future reality.

Human beings were designed to be problem-solvers, and our education drives us to focus on solving the math problem or training our brain via repetition to remember the important dates in history. But the true problem is twofold: it includes both the way we were trained to focus on the problem, and the lack of training in using our minds to create our reality.

Each of us not only creates our individual reality with our thoughts, we also collectively create the reality of the larger sphere—in our community, our society, and our global network. Using random number generators and the collaboration of laboratories all over the world, Dean Radin, PhD, Senior Scientist at The Institute of Noetic Sciences, has demonstrated repeatedly that when people all over the world are focused on a single event—the opening of the Olympics, for example—the shared field represented by the random number generator becomes more coherent. Radin points out, that although we may not be able to influence the outcomes of events very powerfully as individuals, we may be able to achieve that influence as a group or collective. I wonder sometimes what would happen if we all stopped focusing on the negative, and began to focus on what's positive about life. I bet reality could change pretty quickly.

So how can we do that? As human beings trained to focus on problems day in and day out, over and over, with an intensity born of fear that we will not be able to solve them, we simply need to retrain our thinking. We've learned a huge habit of focusing on all the problems in our daily lives that we haven't gotten around to solving, or that are unsolvable at the moment. But this practice creates problems so rut-bound that it takes an earthquake of positive energy to move them. We need to break our thinking habits and create new ones based on the old adage, "What you focus on expands."

"Positive thinking" itself is well and good, but the problem with affirmations, in my experience, is that I always feel like I'm trying to lie to myself. If I say to myself, "I have $100,000 in the bank" and I don't, my brain won't let me believe it because part of me knows it's just not true.

I can get around my brain a bit by adding a feeling state, asking "What would it feel like to have $100,000 in the bank?" and then trying to fan the tiny flame of feeling of what that might be like. But positive thinking doesn't really address the issue of what to do when bad things are happening, or when we're having difficult experiences.

What gets in the way of our being able to create our reality is our habit of focusing on problems, or, for some people, focusing on what's negative or difficult in their lives. For some of us, it's just more comfortable to focus on what's challenging or what isn't working than it is to focus on what makes us happy. For years, my own difficult childhood made it feel safer somehow to not have much going well in my life, because having problems kept me safe when I was small. When I was in a good space, I usually got in trouble or someone else got upset. Negative thinking is simply a habit that needs to be broken.

You can grow your own economy by retraining your brain to ignore the negative and focus on the positive. The stock market is a good example. If you have any interest at all in the market, you probably watch it avidly, and at times, fearfully. Every time you log on to your favorite financial site or watch the Dow Jones numbers on the news, your focus probably gets more intense as the numbers fall. And that continues to create the reality in which the numbers fall. But if you smile and go on your merry way when the numbers are rising, they usually continue to rise.

I imagine the original expectation when we became problem-solvers was that the worse things got, the more we would be doing to fix the problem. But you can't fix the economy by yourself, so every time you tune in, if the news is not so good, the fear barometer goes up a little more, and the picture of a bad economy gets a little more entrenched. As this happens collectively, we're all creating a worsening economy together with our collective thoughts and expectations.

So the first step to growing your own economy is to break that habit, and *stop* focusing on the economy (or any other problem you're having) when the news is bad. This is the more difficult step, because it requires vigilance. It requires *noticing* when you're doing the same old thing, and *stopping* yourself once you notice it.

Step two in growing your own economy is a little easier, and you can implement it right along with step one: when something positive happens, even if it's minute, focus on that with all your might. You've probably heard that what you focus on expands. Step two is a direct test of that theory.

If you notice that the unemployment rate went down by 0.8% since the week before, you might be tempted to say "Whoopee do," and go back to focusing on how bad it's been lately. But the fact is, when the jobless rate goes down by even 0.8%, it's a *window of opportunity* to change reality—for all of us to change our collective reality.

If you take even a few moments to focus on the fact that more people have jobs this week than last week, you've added some fertilizer to help the economy grow. And when the Dow goes down a hundred points or the jobless rate rises, ignore it. You can't do anything about it yourself except in the way you're thinking, and after all, if you want to grow tulips, and there are some weeds springing up around the tulips, you don't sit there and focus on how the weeds are going to outgrow your tulips and how strong they are and how tenacious they are and that if they continue to grow they'll probably kill the tulips. You pull them out, throw them away, forget about them, and feed the tulips so they become stronger and more beautiful. What you focus on expands.

By ignoring the negative news when you can't do anything about it, and focusing on the positive news, even if it's minor, you're beginning to grow your own economy. You can make changes begin to happen with just a few repetitions of "ignore the negative, focus on the positive." Focus on the excitement you feel when things are going right, rather than the angst you feel when they're not.

Here's a review, because right now your brain has probably processed the ideas behind the two steps, and then started to go back to its old habit. It takes *habitual retraining* to overcome a habit. Step one: ignore the negative, or what it is that you don't want. Step two: give any positive events, no matter how small, your good attention for at least a few moments, longer if you can.

During those moments, tell yourself that you look forward to even more positive change. And by the way, if you begin to feel unsafe or "wrong" somehow when you focus on the positive with the hopes of creating a better life or more solid investments, you need to do some thinking about where that came from and how you can overcome it—who told you that?

Were they right about everything?—or it will remain an obstacle to moving forward for a long time. I know. I've been there. A habit of negative thinking is usually based on a person's history, and usually means that a belief system needs to be examined, or something from the past needs to be acknowledged and let go of.

I'm not suggesting that you just ignore all the problems in your life. If there's something in your life that's just not working for you, and there is a solution, by all means get to work on that problem, and do what you can to alleviate it. It's the problems that we can't solve as individuals that are most amenable to this process.

Here's a note about what to watch out for: We tend to discount events that aren't part of our daily experience—for instance, if someone gives us a pat on the back for a job well done, and we're not used to that, our brain will tend to discount it as a part of our larger reality, because it happens so rarely. It's an anomaly that doesn't fit into the brain's negative filing system.

But in order to create a better life or a growing economy, we need to *focus on the anomaly* instead of the usual stuff. This is that *window of opportunity* that offers a possible road to a new experience of reality. It takes a little practice—it's much easier to just go along in the same old rut, ignoring a small new experience. But by focusing on the small green shoots of positive experience that show up in your reality, or the small positive events that contribute to a better economy, you can grow them into a rich garden of positive energy in your life.

And while you're at it, you can do the same with world problems: focus on every small, positive event that you notice, and remove your focus from the huge problems that you can't do anything about. If you can be a part of the solution, spend some energy doing that, but if it's a problem you can't solve yourself, let it go and reach out for what's good. Not only can you grow your own economy, you can grow your own world if you retrain your thinking.

What Are You Sending to the Government?

On first thought, you might think, I'm sending a portion of my income, and they're not doing a very good job with it. We send off our tax forms, on paper or electronically, and we send our opinions in the form of votes. But what are we sending to the government every day?

As I've mentioned numerous times, our thoughts create our reality. And our collective thoughts have even more power to create our reality. I find myself, when I think of our president and the government, sending very negative energy: "Oh, things are really messed up!" "I can't believe they're doing that!" There are probably millions of people in this country sending creative thoughts to the Universe suggesting that our government is really bad..... Doesn't it seem like it would make the situation worse?

And then there's whatever latest war is dominating the news: if we hear that 500 people died as a car bomb exploded in a residential area in a country overrun by war, we visualize that: 500 people dying—and so the next day, our visualization comes true and more people die in the war, which creates the same thing the next day, and recreates the same thing the next day, and that continues as well.....

We're often not aware of how much reality we're creating *just by seeing things as they currently are*. Every time we send a thought that validates the current reality, we're recreating what's happening, even if we're trying to change things or move forward in a positive way.

I remember a TV show called "Commander in Chief," which offered a more positive vision of what our president and government could be like. That's the right idea! By creating a new vision, we can change the reality that our country is collectively creating.

I have come to believe that one of the keys to creating a new reality is not necessarily to paste a picture of what you want to be happening over the picture of current reality—because it's pretty difficult to know that our government is in trouble at the same time that you say to yourself, "I create a wonderful, democratic, caring government" or whatever it is that you're looking for. Your logical mind will keep bringing you back to, "But right now, it's really in trouble!"

Instead, we need to take a step *beyond* current reality in our creative thinking—if every time we heard about a new government blunder, we thought, "Boy, was that a mistake! But I send love and light that those involved may learn from that mistake and find a better way" or however you want to phrase it, change would begin to happen, even if it's on a very small level.

When you find yourself thinking about the government (or anything else) in a negative way, take an extra second or two to take that next step and say to yourself, "But that only means the problems are becoming clearer so that they can be resolved. I send the creative energy of resolution."

I truly believe that our current reality, and in fact the events of the last two decades, are reflecting the shattering and dissolving of the old way of being so that a new way of being can rise from the ashes. I believe that the light of truth is beginning to shine, in some ways for the first time, into the dark corners of our corporate and religious worlds, to illuminate the corruption of the government. As our collective consciousness evolves to a higher vibration, whatever is not in accord with that higher truth we're reaching for is falling away, rotting, beginning to crumble before the light of truth.

Let us view the world as undergoing a healing process rather than becoming more and more difficult to live in. When healing happens, there is often a rather difficult period before things get better, and if we believe the difficulty is just part of the healing process, then it will be so.

I encourage you, as you go about your daily life, to develop the habit of adding a positive spin to any negative thought you happen to find yourself thinking. Take that second step, and together we can begin to create our own reality.

Writing Prompts

For your edification and possible enjoyment—and maybe even some inspiration for writing—here are some of the writing prompts which gave rise to many of the pieces in this book.

Life is a Whoopee Cushion
Love is a Strange Animal
Comfort Foods
Animals Like Us
Giraffodils
There's a Shark in My Colloquialism
The Dark Side of Spring
Madness, Magic, and Mayhem
Half-false, half-true
90% Stupidity
A Clean Slate
Where the Tame and Wild Meet
Psychobiography
The Great Discovery
Tibet
Screened from View
Anger in a Nutshell
I Am From...

About the Author

A former actress who appeared Off-Broadway and on the daytime drama Guiding Light, Katherine Mayfield is the author of the award-winning memoir *The Box of Daughter: Healing the Authentic Self*; a self-help book on recovering from a dysfunctional family, *Stand Your Ground: How to Cope with a Dysfunctional Family and Recover from Trauma*; a guide to recovery from bullying for teens and adults, called *Bullied: Why You Feel Bad Inside and What to Do About It*; two books on the acting business: *Smart Actors, Foolish Choices* and *Acting A to Z*; both published by Back Stage Books; a book of poetry, *The Box of Daughter & Other Poems*; and a series of Kindle books on dysfunctional families.

Ms. Mayfield has presented writing workshops in New Hampshire, Maines and Massachusetts, and teaches memoir-writing classes online. She blogs on dysfunctional families on her website, www.TheBoxofDaughter.com.

Websites:
www.TheBoxofDaughter.com
www.Katherine-Mayfield.com

Social Media:
Twitter: K_Mayfield
Facebook: KatherineMayfieldauthor

Credits:

"How to Make Monkey Mind Work for You" originally appeared on TinyBuddha.com

"Lunar Disconnect," "The Long-Awaited Rebirth" and "To Everything There is a Season" originally appeared in the *Montague Reporter*, Montague, MA

"This is the Year for Me" originally appeared in *Sasee* magazine

CPSIA information can be obtained
at www.ICGtesting.com
Printed in the USA
LVHW021520070920
665245LV00019B/2397